Dear Parent:
Your child's love of reading starts here!

Every child learns to read in a different way and at his or her own speed. Some go back and forth between reading levels and read favorite books again and again. Others read through each level in order. You can help your young reader improve and become more confident by encouraging his or her own interests and abilities. From books your child reads with you to the first books he or she reads alone, there are I Can Read Books for every stage of reading:

SHARED READING
Basic language, word repetition, and whimsical illustrations, ideal for sharing with your emergent reader

BEGINNING READING
Short sentences, familiar words, and simple concepts for children eager to read on their own

READING WITH HELP
Engaging stories, longer sentences, and language play for developing readers

READING ALONE
Complex plots, challenging vocabulary, and high-interest topics for the independent reader

I Can Read Books have introduced children to the joy of reading since 1957. Featuring award-winning authors and illustrators and a fabulous cast of beloved characters, I Can Read Books set the standard for beginning readers.

A lifetime of discovery begins with the magical words **"I Can Read!"**

Visit www.icanread.com for information
on enriching your child's reading experience.

In memory of Keith Roma,
Patrol 2, New York Fire Patrol
—L.D.

To the first responders who
gave up their lives on 9/11.
Their selfless act of bravery
still amazes me.
—C.E.

I Can Read® and I Can Read Book® are trademarks of HarperCollins Publishers.
I Want to Be a Firefighter
Copyright © 2022 by HarperCollins Publishers
All rights reserved. Printed in the United States of America.
No part of this book may be used or reproduced in any manner whatsoever without written permission except in the case of brief quotations embodied in critical articles and reviews. For information address HarperCollins Children's Books, a division of HarperCollins Publishers, 195 Broadway, New York, NY 10007.
www.icanread.com

Library of Congress Control Number: 2021948123
ISBN 978-0-06-298961-1 (trade bdg.) — ISBN 978-0-06-298962-8 (pbk.)

22 23 24 25 26 LSCC 10 9 8 7 6 5 4 3 2 1
❖
First Edition

I Can Read!

1 BEGINNING READING

I Want to Be a
Firefighter

by Laura Driscoll
pictures by Catalina Echeverri

HARPER
An Imprint of HarperCollinsPublishers

"Fire!" my twin brother, Max, shouts.

We have to rescue Cat

from the top floor of the building.

"Mia!" Max shouts to me.

"Raise the ladder!"

I get the ladder in place.

Max shouts directions.

"A little to the right!

Higher!

There!"

7

Soon Cat is safe and sound.

"I did it!" Max says.

"No, I did!" I say.

"My ladder and I!"

Max crosses his arms.

Which one of us saved the day?

"We will find out

at school today," I say.

It is Fire Safety Day!

There is a fire truck

outside our school!

A bunch of firefighters step out.

Some are wearing fire gear.

Some are wearing uniforms.

"We are from Fire District One,"

says a firefighter.

"I am the fire captain.

I am in charge of our station

and I give orders

when we go to a fire."

Max looks at me.

"I told you," he says.

A different firefighter
gives us a tour of the fire truck.
"I am the engineer," he says.
"I drive the truck,
set up the hoses,
and raise the ladder."

Max and I look at all the controls.

I nudge him.

"See?" I whisper.

"Very important."

We get to try on
a firefighter's jacket.
It is super heavy!

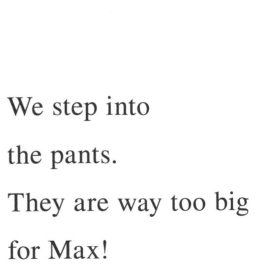

We step into
the pants.
They are way too big
for Max!

16

Another firefighter shows us
the medical kit.

"We don't just put out fires,"
this firefighter says.
"We race to help
in all kinds of emergencies,
so we need to know first aid."

Now Max and I look at each other.

All firefighters help people

who are hurt.

That's really important.

Next we meet the fire investigator.

"My job is to figure out

how a fire started," he says.

The investigator's partner is a dog.

The dog can sniff out clues.

Then we meet a fire marshal.

He fights fires before they happen!

In new buildings,
he checks the smoke alarms,

the sprinklers,

and the fire exits.

"I make sure every building
is safe," the fire marshal says.

"Not all fires are in buildings,"

one firefighter says.

She shows us some photos.

We see her battling

a forest fire.

24

Wildland firefighters
use parachutes or helicopters
to get to fires in rugged areas.

Airport rescue firefighters
work at airports.
They have skills to help
with airplane emergencies.

Some firefighters put out fires

that start from dangerous—

or hazardous—materials.

They are called HazMat firefighters.

They wear special clothing

for extra protection.

The fire captain talks to us
about fire safety at home.
He points at our helmets.

28

"Do you two want to be firefighters?"

he asks.

Max and I nod.

"What kind?" the fire captain asks.

I do not know what to say.

I look at Max.

"There are so many!" Max says.

"And they are all important," I add.

Meet the Firefighters

Firefighter
A rescuer that puts out fires and gives emergency medical help

Fire captain
The person who is in charge of a fire station and at the scene of a fire

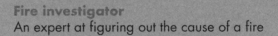

Engineer
A firefighter who drives the fire truck, puts up the ladder, and makes sure the hoses can deliver enough water to put out the fire

Fire investigator
An expert at figuring out the cause of a fire

Fire marshal
A member of the fire department or city government who makes sure buildings are firesafe

Wildland firefighter
A firefighter who puts out and prevents forest fires and grass fires

Airport rescue firefighter
A firefighter who puts out airplane fires and rescues people from airplanes

HazMat firefighter
A firefighter who puts out fires that start from dangerous material